The Craig Duncan Master Fiddle Solo Collection

MW00851572

3 4 5 6 7 8 9 0

Visit us on the Web at http://www.melbay.com — E-mail us at email@melbay.com

Craig Duncan, has been the featured instrumentalist on over fifty record albums, with sales in excess of three million. He is a member of the National Fiddler's Hall of Fame, Who's Who in Music and Musicians and is recognized internationally for his numerous books and arrangements of fiddle music published by Mel Bay Publications. He has produced numerous recordings for the gift shop market in a variety of musical styles. As a hammered dulcimer player, he is known for his work on Green Hill's *Country Mountain* series as well as Brentwood Music's *Smoky Mountain* series. He is active in the Nashville music industry as an instrumentalist, contractor, producer and arranger.

Table of Contents

This collection includes the most frequently played tunes in old time fiddle contests as well as the most popular bluegrass, square dance and country tunes heard throughout the United States. The performance length arrangements of the contest tunes include standard as well as challenging variations on hoedowns, rags, polkas, show pieces and waltzes. The bluegrass style tunes include standard breakdowns and tunes by Bill Monroe, Kenny Baker, Chubby Wise and Vassar Clements as well as hornpipes, reels and barn burning showstoppers. This "encyclopedia" of fiddle tunes and variations spotlights American popular fiddle music as played by the great fiddlers of our time.

Ace of Spades

This is a three part Texas style contest breakdown with a final variation of the first part closing the tune. It is played at a medium tempo.

Angeline the Baker

Oldtime-tradtional

Rugged oldtime fiddling with a heavy beat is the style of this tune often heard with clawhammer banjo. The open strings heard throughout the tune are characteristic of this style of fiddling.

Allentown Polka

Polka-traditional

Polkas are sometimes used as the tune of choice in oldtime fiddle contests. This tune is unusual in that the second part uses the same chord progression as the first part one whole step higher.

Arkansas Traveler

Oldtime - traditional

A double stop drone style section opens this arrangement of Arkansas Traveler. The second part uses "Georgia Bow" to add a driving lilt to the tune. The third section is a high octave variation of the first part. The fourth section is an oldtime variation on the second part. It uses fewer melody notes with an added drone and shuffle bowing, which lends an old time square dance feel.

Ashokan Farewell

Jay Ungar

Jay Ungar wrote and recorded this tune on a *Fiddle Fever* album in 1983. It was used later as background music on the PBS Civil War series and a fiddle "hit" was born. Although many fiddle waltzes are played with swing eighth notes, this tune is played with even eighths in the style of a Celtic air. Measures 33-64 offer a double stop version of the tune. The original was recorded with three fiddles.

Back Up and Push

Traditional

This tune is played up tempo with a bluesy feel to the first part. The slide in measure seven from the Bb to the A should be done with the fourth finger. The second part of the tune is classic double shuffle.

Beaumont Rag

Rag-traditional

Ragtime tunes are played at a medium tempo with a slight swing. The slides add a bluesy feel. The first, second and fifth parts of this arrangement are all variations on the original theme. The third part is a standard section, played in fifth position from measure 33-44, with the shift down coming on an open string. The fourth section is a double shuffle variation, and should be altered or omitted if played in a contest.

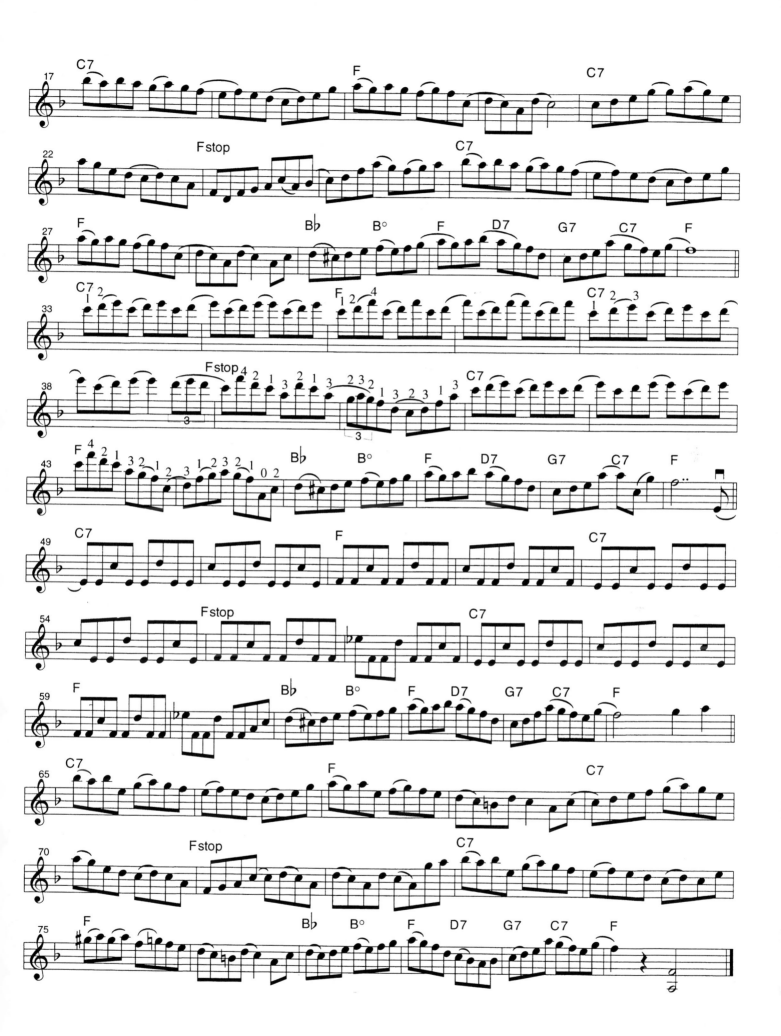

Bill Cheatham

Oldtime - Bluegrass

Often played by bluegrass fiddlers, this tune comes out of the Southern tradition of hard driving fiddle tunes. It is a two part tune presented here with variations. The first part is measures 1-8 with variations in measures 7-16, 33-40 and 41-48. The second part is measures 17-24, with variations in measures 25-32, 49-56 and 57-64.

14

Billy in the Lowground

Hoedown-traditional

Contest players have taken this two part traditional oldtime square dance tune and added many variations. The chord progression can be the same for both parts, however, in this arrangement the F chord is used in the second part to give contrast from the A minor of the first part. Bluegrass fiddlers often use this chord progression. The arrangement here is twice through the tune with variations.

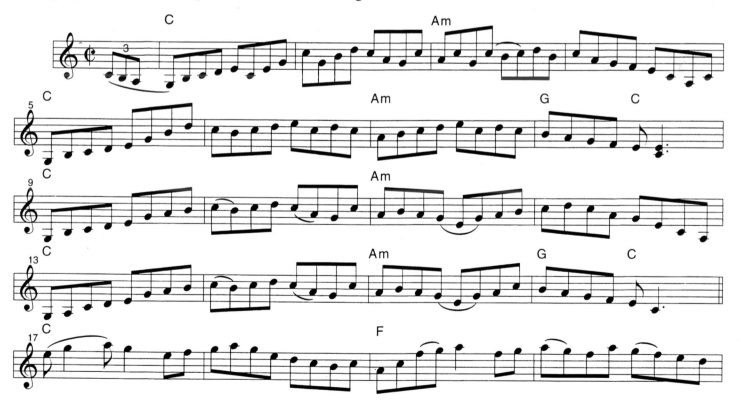

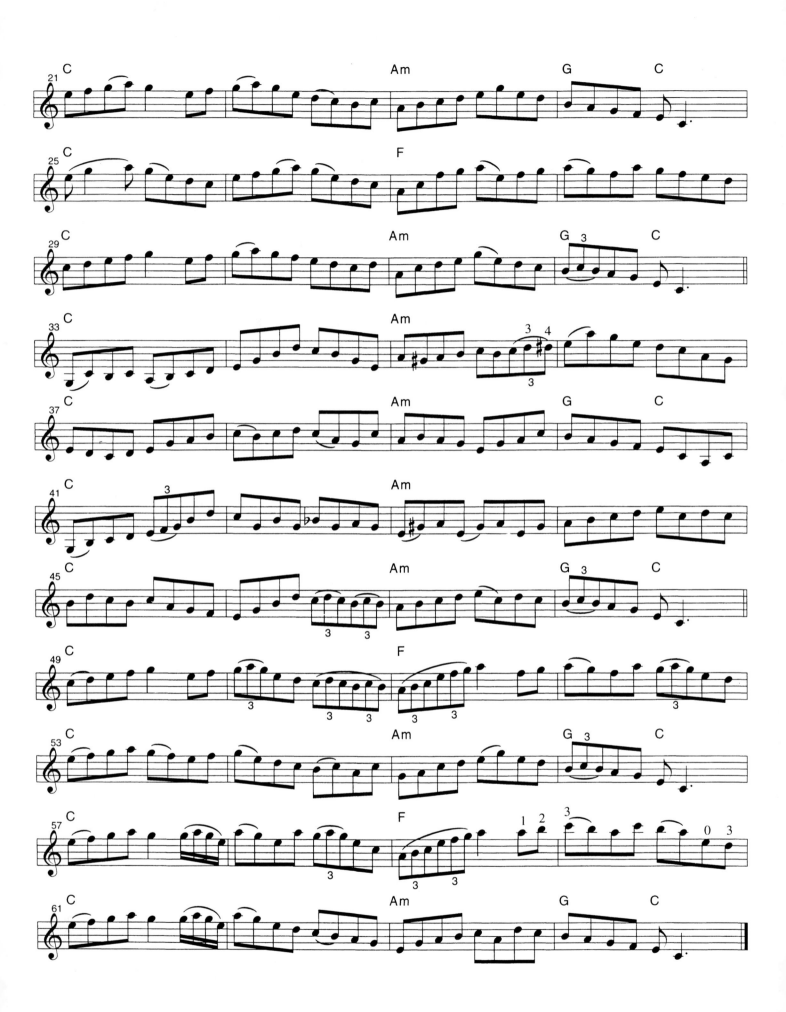

Bitter Creek

Contest hoedown - traditional

This is a two part tune presented with variations. The basic chords are in this arrangement, although the tune works well with Texas swing accompaniment.

Black and White Rag

Rag - traditional

Measures 1-17 present the main melody to this tune. The second part is found in measures 18-33 with a variation in 34-65. A third section is in measures 66-81. When the tune is played for an extended length, the form is typically AABBAABBCA. The first section is used to close the tune.

18

Black Eyed Suzie

D.C. al Fine

Bluegrass-traditional

Paul Warren performed this tune with Flatt & Scruggs. There is a spoken lyric that is done between the instrumental verses. 1. Black Eyed Suzie went to town and all she wore was a gingham gown.
Chorus Hey, black eyed Suzie, Ho, black eyed Suzie, Hey, black eyed Suzie, Ho, black eyed Suzie,
2. Black eyed Suzie long and tall, sleeps in the kitchen with her feet in the hall. Chorus
3. All I want to make me happy is a sweet little boy to call me pappy. Chorus
4. I love my wife, I love my baby, I love my biscuits sopped in gravy. Chorus

Blackberry Blossom

Arthur Smith - Hoedown

Fiddlin' Arthur Smith from Tennessee wrote this two part tune which has evolved into a popular bluegrass and square dance feature. This arrangement includes three times through the tune with variations written out for each section. Measures 97-101 give the standard ending to the tune.

Black Mountain Rag

tune open strings

The fiddle should be re-tuned as indicated. The pitches written in the music here are the fingerings to be used, not the actual notes heard. This tune comes from the Cumberland Plateau region of Tennessee. It is quite an interesting tune to play and to listen to because of the cross tuning and the special effects. LH stands for left hand pizzicato.

Bully of the Town

Old Time - Bluegrass

It is unusual to have a tune that has a 12 measure A part and a 16 measure B part. That may be the reason that the first part is usually repeated and the second is not. This is a Southern tune played in the style of tunes like *Down Yonder* and *Alabama Jubilee*.

Boil Them Cabbage Down

Hoedown - traditional

This hoedown is one of the first tunes many fiddlers learn. Several variations along with the verse are found in this version. When playing the double shuffle variation in measures 33-48, the left hand should make the chord changes (including fourth finger) on the downbeat letting the bow work emphasis the written pitches.

Bonaparte's Retreat

Traditional

Measures 1-8 and 17-24 are variations on the first part of this tune. Measures 9-16, 25-32 and 41-48 are
variations on the second part. Measures 33-40 come from a bridge section in the vocal version of the tune.

Brilliancy

Hoedown - Old Time

Brilliancy comes from the Texas contest tradition as is evident by the chord structure given. It is played at a medium tempo. There are three parts, with variations, followed by final variations on the first part.

27

Cattle in the Cane

Bluegrass-Southeast-traditional

In this version of *Cattle in the Cane,* the two parts alternate between A minor and A major. The tune is played with a driving rhythm.

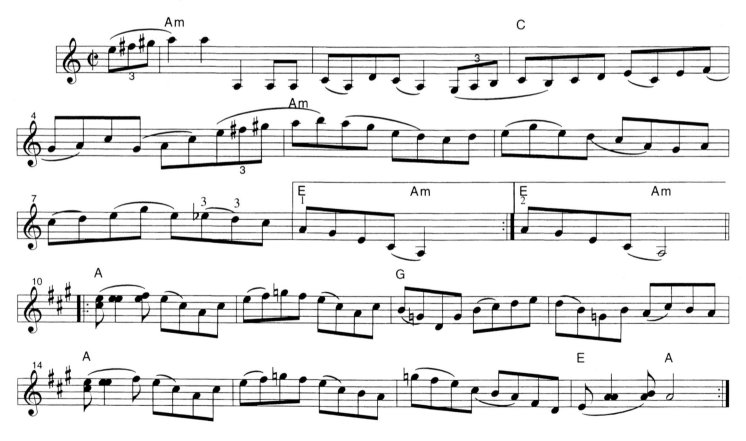

Cattle in the Cane

Although the notes are much the same in the Texas style version as in the Southeastern version, the B part is played in E minor instead of A. As is typical of Texas style fiddling, this version should be played with more bounce and less drive than the other version.

29

Calgary Polka
Gaudette Polka

Polka - traditional

This is a two part tune which requires a bit of third position work. The shifts are most easily done while playing an open E string. Although the fingering in measure 43 is a bit unorthodox, it makes the section easier to play.

Champagne Polka

Traditional

This tune has two parts, with a pizzicato variation in measure 33-42. The final two sections present a "perpetual motion" type variation including some double shuffle work.

Chancellor's Waltz

Contest Waltz-traditional

Texas contest style playing is the background for this waltz which has an ABCA form. The first part is measures 1-16, the second is 17-32 and the third 33-48. Measures 49-64 are a variation on the first part. The eighth notes are played with a swing feel.

Cherokee Shuffle

Traditional

This Southern hoedown uses a drone fourth finger and shuffle bowing. It should be played up tempo.

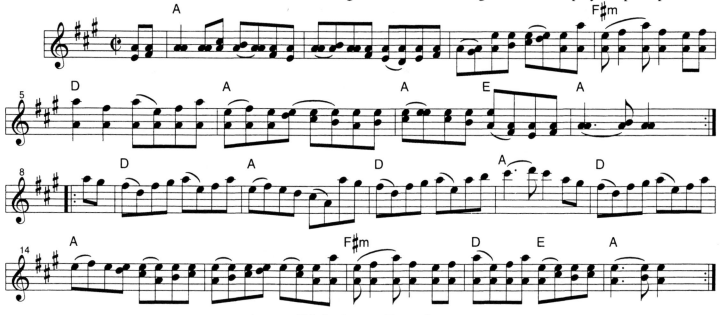

Chicken Reel

Old Time - traditional

The F natural to F sharp slide should be performed as definite pitches with a slide between them. After the third finger is put in place in measure six, it should remain down for the rest of the measure.

Chinky Pin

Chinquapin, Too Young to Marry

Old Time - traditional

The origin of this tune is blurred, as *Too Young to Marry* and *My Love She's But a Lassie* are Scotch Irish tunes very similar to this one. The current name must have come from the mispronuciation of Chinquapin.

Choctaw

This is a two part tune with variations. The first measure and similar places can be played in second position, shifting back on the first note (open E string) of the next measure.

Cincinnati Rag

Rag-traditional

The first part of *Cincinnati Rag* follows a standard 6-2-5-1 chord progression. However, the tune truly establishes its identity in the second part, going from the E chord in measure 17 to the C chord in measure 19. Variations on the two parts are found in measures 33-64.

Cotton Patch Rag

Rag - traditional

There are seven variations on the tune based on one harmonic progression. This has become a "jam" tune for oldtime and contest fiddlers. Follow the bowings and fingerings carefully in measures 81-96. This is a very interesting section which alters the harmonies to C6 - F7b9 - G9 - C.

Cottoneyed Joe:1

This is the tune which goes with the Cottoneyed Joe line dance.

Traditional

Cottoneyed Joe:2

This tune from the southeastern mountain tradition is often performed with a vocal. A heavily sequenced version of the tune was a pop hit in the 1990's.

Traditional Southeastern

Cripple Creek

Traditional

Cripple Creek is a bluegrass standard, played both in the key of A and the key of G. Almost every banjo player knows this tune. This version gives the basic melody followed by a typical variation.

Cuckoo's Nest

Hoedown-traditional

This is a two part tune with written out variations on each eight measure section. Measures 33-64 present even more variations. This arrangement is a hybrid of oldtime and contest fiddle styles.

41

Dill Pickle Rag

Rag - Charles Johnson 1907

...ed at a medium tempo with a bounce. In the Ragtime Era, 1900-1920, these ...hth notes. Later, musicians began to swing the eighths. You can play it either ... you wish to be. *Dill Pickle Rag* has three sections and should end with a

Fine

D.C. al Fine

Additional Variations

43

Don't Let Your Deal Go Down

Rag - traditional

This is a ragtime tune based entirely on a 6 - 2 - 5 - 1 progression. Measures 81 and 90 are "extra measures" based on a rendition by Benny Thomasson.

Done Gone

The first section of this oldtime version of *Done Gone* and the bluegrass version that follows is essentially the same. However, this version has two more sections, making it a three part tune which ends with a restatement of the first part.

Done Gone

Bluegrass fiddler Kenny Baker is the inspiration for this version of *Done Gone*. It is a two part tune.

Durham's Bull

Bluegrass

Fast is an understatement for the tempo this tune is usually played. Drone notes are often added, giving the tune a real hard driving sound. This is done by placing the first finger on the G and D strings and bowing both strings throughout measures 1-2, bowing the D and A strings together during measures 3-4, etc.

Down Yonder

Traditional

This is a forty measure country instrumental followed by a fiddle style variation. When performing *Down Yonder* with a band, it is common parctice for instruments other than the lead to play the two phrases marked "echo" (measures 23-24 and 63-64).

Draggin' the Bow

Rag - Kurt Massey

This arrangement presents an intro and main theme followed by two variations. The chromatic licks in measures 11-12 are played by sliding the fingers from the flat notes up to the key notes with open strings between each set of fingerings.

Durang's Hornpipe

Hornpipe - traditional

This is a two part tune with variations. Measures 1-16, 33-48 and 65-80 make up the variations on the first part. Measures 17-32 and 49-64 make up the variations on the second part.

Dusty Miller

Dusty Miller is a four part tune played in both contest and bluegrass styles. The chords in this arrangement are typical of contest backup. When played as a bluegrass tune, the only chords used are A, G and E, with the first two parts using a G chord in the second measure of each line. This gives a very modal tone to the tune.

52

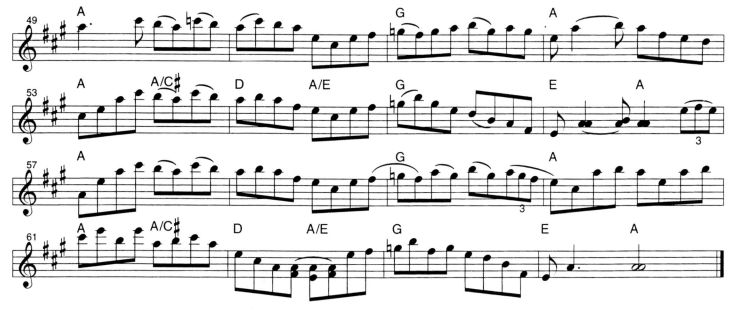

East Tennessee Blues

Traditional

Although called a blues, this tune is played at a medium fast tempo with even eighth notes. The slides in the second part lend a bluesy feel.

Eighth of January

Old Time - traditional

The Battle of New Orleans, a song written by Jimmy Driftwood, is based on this melody which was written to commemorate the defeat of the British on January 8, 1814. It is a two part tune, presented here with a variation on each part.

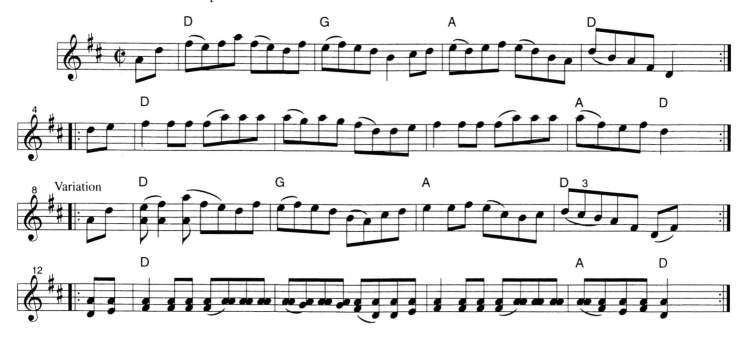

Fiddler's Dream

Traditional hoedown

The first part of this tune is rather straight forward. However, the second part has a five measure phrase followed by a three measure phrase. This gives a genuine old time feeling to the tune.

54

Festival Waltz

Kenny Baker

This beautiful waltz written and performed by Kenny Baker is played with swing eighth notes. Full, long bow strokes should be used to give the tune a flowing character.

Fiddler's Waltz

This is an unusual tune, having five distinct sections. Fingerings are marked to help with the necessary shifting. The tune is played at a medium tempo with semi-classical approach.

Fireman's Reel

Traditional

This is a typical up tempo two part reel.

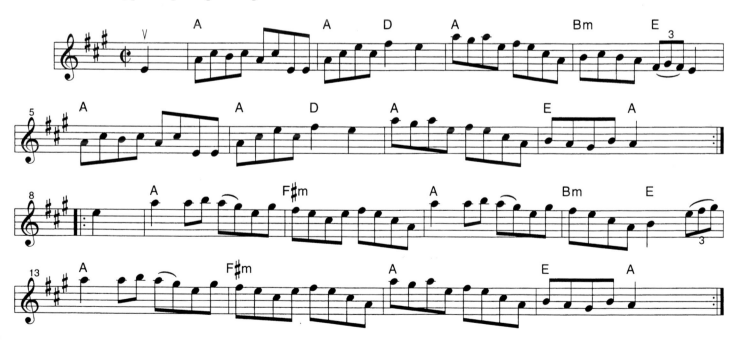

Fifty Years Ago Waltz

Contest Waltz

As is customary in fiddle waltzes, the eighth notes in this tune are played in swing style. The slides indicated are to be performed in a subtle manner. Measures 33-34 are performed by setting the fingering and rocking the bow between the G string and the D and A strings.

Fire on the Mountain

Old Time-traditional

High energy hoedown fiddling characterizes the style of this tune. It is often played with drone strings sounding - bowing the A and E strings while fingering the pitches written for the first part, and bowing the D and A strings or D and G strings while playing the second part. A peculiar quirk to the tune is found in the last two measures, which seem to be extra, but are in fact performed with each repetition of the tune.

Fisher's Hornpipe

Traditional

The original key of this popular hornpipe is found here. Many fiddlers play this tune in D, however, it loses some of its charm when the licks are altered to accommodate the key change. The third part was not an original section of the tune, but was added at a later date. Some fiddlers use it, others do not.

*optional part

Flop Eared Mule

Oldtime - traditional

This tune is played in both the keys of G and D. In performance, the two parts are played by each musician, with a final statement of the first part ending the tune. A high octave variation is found in measures 17-34.

Forked Deer

Traditional

The first part of *Forked Deer* is very standard from player to player. There are many variations on the second part. The second part here features a drone A and combines ideas from many sources.

Gardenia Waltz

Johnny Gimble

Johnny Gimble wrote this double stop showcase waltz. Because of the beauty of the tune and its difficulty, it has become a contest standard. It requires quite a bit of left hand gymnastics, so the double stops should be studied carefully to learn the best approach for your personal style of playing.

Georgiana Moon

Waltz-traditional

One of the most popular fiddle waltz patterns opens this tune: starting on the key note and descending by steps, with a 1 - 3 minor - 6 minor - 1 chord progression. Although many guitarists play a G chord in measure 28, it is really a G+ because of the Eb in the fiddle. Long smooth bow strokes should be used.

62

German Waltz

Waltz - traditional

Swing eighth notes are used throughout this waltz and the sixteenth notes are played like grace notes rather than even sixteenths. This is a three part tune with a final variation on the first part.

Get Up John

Traditional

This is a four part oldtime hoedown. It is played with a hard driving shuffle style bowing to create a southern square dance feel.

Golden Eagle Hornpipe

Traditional

This hornpipe is played at a medium tempo, using seperate bow strokes except for the two places indicated. The style of the tune is more like Scottish and Canadian fiddling than square dance or Texas contest style.

Golden Slippers

Old Time - traditional

This popular Southern fiddle tune is the melody to a spiritual. It makes a good twin fiddle number.

Goodbye Liza Jane

Traditional

Two versions of *Goodbye Liza Jane* are given here. The first presents the basic melody. Measures 18-34 give standard fiddling treatment to the melody.

Grandfather Polka
Clarinet Polka

Polka - traditional

The *Grandfather Polka* is the same tune as the *Clarinet Polka,* only in a different key and played with idiomatic fiddle licks. The *Clarinet Polka* is usually played in Bb. This version begins with two statements of the first part, followed by the B part in the key of D. The first part is played again, followed by the C part in the key of C. The tune closes with the first part, giving the overall form - AABACA

66

D.S. al Fine

Grey Eagle

Contest Hoedown - traditional

Contest, bluegrass and oldtime fiddlers all play their versions of *Grey Eagle*. The first part presents the tune in a square dance style. Measures 18, 22-23 and 30-31 are more easily played in third position. Measures 33-48 is a contest style variation on the first part. Measures 49-64 is a contest style variation on the second part. The third part of the tune is found in measures 65-80 and the fourth in 81-96. A final variation on the first part closes the tune.

Herman's Rag

Rag-traditional

This is a two part Texas contest tune with variations. It is played at a medium tempo and is another example of a ragtime tune being based on a 6 - 2 - 5 - 1 chord progression. The tune is attributed to Herman Johnson.

Goodnight Waltz

Waltz - traditional

This waltz comes from the contest tradition, with its many turns and chromatic licks. It is played in a smooth, connected style, using long bow strokes.

Hell Among the Yearlings

Contest Style Hoedown

This two part American tune is used as a contest tune as well as a square dance number.

Hell Among the Yearlings

Oldtime-traditional

This version has one major difference from the previous version - the first part is nine measures long. This type of phrasing came from the time when most fiddling was unaccompanied, and the fiddler could stretch phrases at will. It gives a genuine oldtime feel to the tune.

Highland Hornpipe

Traditional

Contest style treatment has been given to this hornpipe. There are two basic sections to the tune, measures 1-8 and 9-16. Measures 17-24 and 41-48 are restatements of the first part. Measures 25-40 offer two different musical ideas. Measures 49-56 are a high octave variation on the first part. The second part is restated in 56-64 and the tune ends with a DC to the first part.

74

D.C. al Fine

Home With the Girls in the Morning

Appalachian - tradtitional

The tradition of this tune is the haunting sound of modal Appalachian fiddling. It is best played with the accompaniment using no thirds in the chords.

Hotfoot

Rag - traditional

This one part ragtime tune is given a contest style theme and variations treatment. It is played at a medium tempo with even eighth notes. Measure 41 is played with a "stutter" bowing. The high C's in measures 5, 49 and 57 are most easily played with an extended fourth finger.

Jack of Diamonds

Traditional

Contest style licks and variations are found throughout this two part, oldtime hoedown. The first part is found in measures 1-8, with variations in measures 9-16, 33-40 and 41-48. The second part is measures 17-24 with variations in 25-32, 49-56 and 57-64.

Jerusalem Ridge

Bill Monroe-Kenny Baker-Bluegrass

Kenny Baker recorded this Bill Monroe tune which has become one of the favorite bluegrass fiddle pieces. It is a four part tune. The guitar and bass usually play the E chord in measure 22 and 26 with a C bass on the first beat and a B bass on the second beat of the measure, walking down to the A on the downbeat of the next measure.

I Don't Love Nobody

Rag - traditional

Originally this tune was played in a bluesy style in the key of C. This is very much a hot lick, contest style arrangement of the tune. Measure 33-40 and 73-80 present a bridge which is often omitted by contest fiddlers.

Jesse Polka

esusito en Chihuahua

Polka-traditional

...n tradition has been incorporated into the standard fiddle repertory.
...final statement of the first part.

Jolie Blonde

Henry Choates - Cajun

Jolie Blonde is the most famous of the Cajun fiddle waltzes and is played by many fiddlers of various backgrounds. Measure 1 is a pickup to the tune. Sometimes the tune is played without the second part- measures 18-32. In the original, it is an instrumental interlude between the vocal verses.

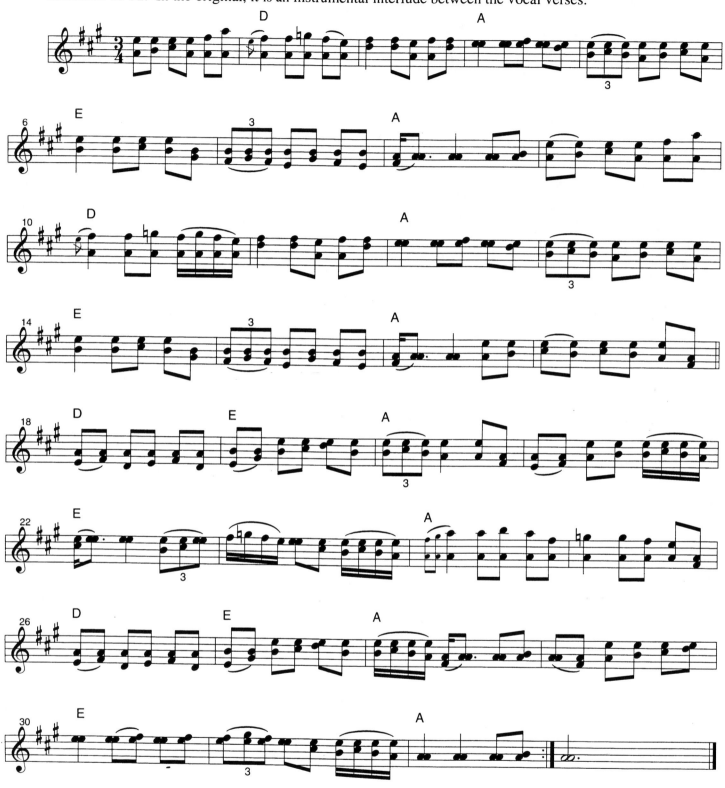

Katy Hill

Old Time-Bluegrass-traditional

This is essentially the same tune as *Sally Johnson,* played in a bluegrass/square dance style. It is a two part tune, that is usually performed faster than *Sally Johnson* and the implied Em chord in measure 4 is played as a G chord.   Measures 17-24 present a standard variation on the first part.

Variations

Kelly's Waltz

Contest - Old Time

Many shifts between third and first positions are required in this waltz showpiece. It is played with swing eighths. The first part is thirty two measures long and is used to begin and end the tune. Three other sixteen measure parts are found between measures 33-80.

Leather Britches

Old-Time

This southern fiddle tune takes its name from dried green beans, which were called "leather britches."

87

Limerock

Show piece -traditional

There are five sections to this tune. The first part is the "signature" part of the tune and occurs in measures 1-16, 33-68 and 129-144. A low octave variation is in measures 97-112. The second part, in the key of D, is in measures 17-32 with a variation in 113-128. The third part, in the key of E, is measures 49-64. The fourth part is measures 65-80 and the fifth part is measures 81-96.

88

Listen to the Mockingbird

Traditional

A nineteenth century popular song is the basis for this fiddling showpiece. The verse melody is in measures
1-8 followed by a variation in 9-16 The chorus of the tune is measures 17-24. Fiddlistic variations follow.
The bird calls are done by sliding the left hand on the strings in imitation of different birds.

91

Lonesome Fiddle Blues

Vassar Clements

Vassar Clements wrote this two part fiddle tune which first appeared on the *Will the Circle Be Unbroken* album in 1972. It quickly became a fiddling standard. The form of the thirty two measure tune is AABA. Measures 33-64 present more Vassar variations.

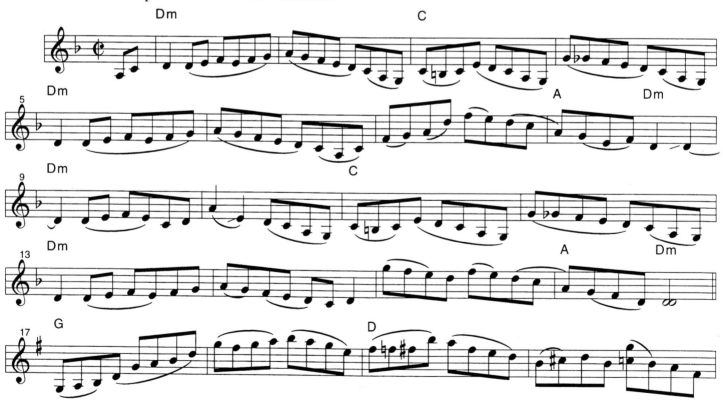

93

Liberty

Old Time - traditional

ce tune.

Lonesome John

Appalachian

The E5 chords (E without a third) and the Dm chords can also be played as G chords in this modal tune.

Lonesome Moonlight Waltz

Bill Monroe

This haunting melody recorded by Bill Monroe and the Bluegrass Boys makes a great twin fiddle tune.

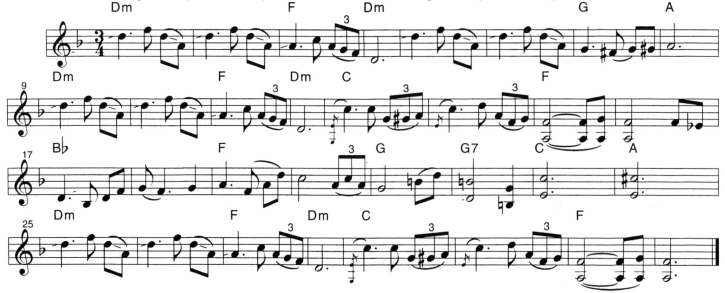

Lost Indian

Oldtime - Bluegrass

This is a two part square dance tune. Measure 1-16 present the basic single note melody. Fiddlers often play the tune with double stops including a drone fourth finger on the G string as found in measures 17-18 and 33-34.

Lost Highway Blues
Lee Highway Blues

Traditional

This tune is played with hard driving energy. The form is rather loose. Measures 1-8 are sometimes repeated. The licks in measures 52-59 are different inversions of D chord fingerings, starting a half step low and sliding up to pitch, with open strings between each set. This technique can be applied in other "jam" situations. The parallel fifths in measures 72-77, 91-94 and 104-107 may sound odd at first hearing, but up to speed in context, they add a hard driving old time flavor.

96

Maiden's Prayer

Traditional

This traditional tune is often associated with Bob Wills. It is a one part tune played in a swing 4/4 time. The basic melody is found in measures 1-16. Measures 17-32 add a few double stops and fiddle licks. Tremolo bowing is used in measures 33-40. A western swing arrangement with extensive use of A6 and D6 chords are found in measures 49-64.

98

Martin's Waltz

A rocking bow lick is used throughout this traditional contest style waltz. It has t̶
ABA form. The bowing should be smooth and connected.

Memory Waltz

Contest waltz - traditional

...with swing eighths. It uses many third position double stops. Measures ...oe played with a Viennese lilt. The DS goes back to measure 49.

Fine

D.S. al Fine

Midnight on the Water

Waltz-Luke Thomasson

Open D tuning drops the E string to a D and the G string to a low D. This tuning was originally used for *Midnight on the Water.* The arrangement here avoids the G string, so the open tuning is accomplished by tuning the E string down to D. The notes written top space E and above will sound one step lower than written.

Miss McLeod's Reel
Hop Light Ladies - Did You ever See the Devil, Uncle Joe?

Old Time-Celtic

Originally a tune from Scotland, this sixteen measure tune is found throughout American fiddling under several different titles. There are three variations of the tune found here.

102

Mississippi Sawyer

Old Time - traditional

A "Mississippi sawyer" is a log floating in the river. This is a two part American square dance tune, presented with a low octave variation on each part in measures 17-32.

Variations

Old Joe Clark

Old Time - traditional

Bluegrass and square dance fiddling are the basis for this version of *Old Joe Clark*. In oldtime versions, the G chord in measure 12 is played as an E, with the fiddler playing an E on the D string instead of a G.

*This page has been
left blank to avoid
awkward page turns*

Over the Waves

Juventino Rosas

Although not originally written as a fiddling tune, *Over the Waves* has become one of the most well known fiddle waltzes. Both parts of the tune are found in this southern style arrangement.

Paddy on the Turnpike

Bluegrass - traditional

The early versions of this tune are in the key of G minor. The tune has now evolved into a two part "jam" tune in G major. Many of the licks beginning in measure 18 are based on Vassar Clements fiddling.

106

Over the Waterfall

Traditional

This two part American tune makes delightful use of the flat seven to four progression in measures 7-8.

Rachel

Traditional

The distinguishing lick in this American square dance tune is measures 9-10 and 13-14.

Red Haired Boy
Little Beggar Man

Traditional - Irish

This tune can be played in a variety of styles, from this bowing to adding drones to hornpipe style dotted rhythms.

Ragtime Annie
Raggedy Ann

Traditional

This tune originally ended in measure 24. The third part, measures 25-33, was added later and is not played by all fiddlers. A nice way to approach this discrepancy is to use the third part only once during the tune as a bridge section.

Optional 3rd part

Fine

D.C. al Fine

Red Wing

Kerry Mills

Kerry Mills wrote this melody to the popular song, *Red Wing,* in 1907. It has become a fiddling classic.

109

Road to Columbus

Bill Monroe - Kenny Baker - Bluegrass

Kenny Baker made this tune a bluegrass fiddle classic. The tempo begins in measure 5, after the ab lib solo fiddle intro. This is a two part tune that is so well defined, repetitions of the tune are usually played without variation.

Rose of Sharon
Rose of Allenvale

Waltz-traditional

Howdy Forrester recorded this two part waltz as *Rose of Sharon,* which it is commonly known as in American fiddle circles. *Rose of Allenvale* is the Scottish name for the tune. Measures 33-48 present a low octave variation of the first part.

Roxanna Waltz

Waltz-Contest-traditional

This southern fiddle waltz is a two part tune, beginning in the key of C. Measure 32 is a pivotal transposition measure to the key of A. Although the tune can be played exclusively in C, this key change gives the tune a lift and the different voicings in the key of A add a new dimension to the tune.

Rubber Dolly

Traditional

This tune is practically the same as *Back Up and Push* played in a different key. The lyric is as follows:
"My mama told me, if I was goody, that she would buy me a rubber dolly.
My sister told her, I kissed a soldier, now she won't buy me a rubber dolly."

Sally Ann *or* Sail Away Ladies

Traditional

This version comes from a West Virginia tradition and includes an Em and a C chord in the first part.
Bluegrass players, particularly banjo players, often use a C instead of the Em.

113

Sally Ann

Contest style fiddling is the basis for this arrangement of *Sally Ann*.

Traditional

Rye Straw

Oldtime - traditional

There are six parts to this oldtime fiddle tune. The first and fourth parts are very similar. The second, third and fifth parts are also similar. The sixth part acts as a bridge back to the beginning.

Sally Goodin

This is the definitive fiddle breakdown. Square dance, bluegrass, oldtime and contest fiddlers all have their versions. This arrangement presents the standard variations plus hot licks from several styles of fiddling.

116

Sally Johnson

Contest Hoedown

This is the epitome of Texas contest style fiddling. Contest style guitar chords are given along with eight variations on the tune.

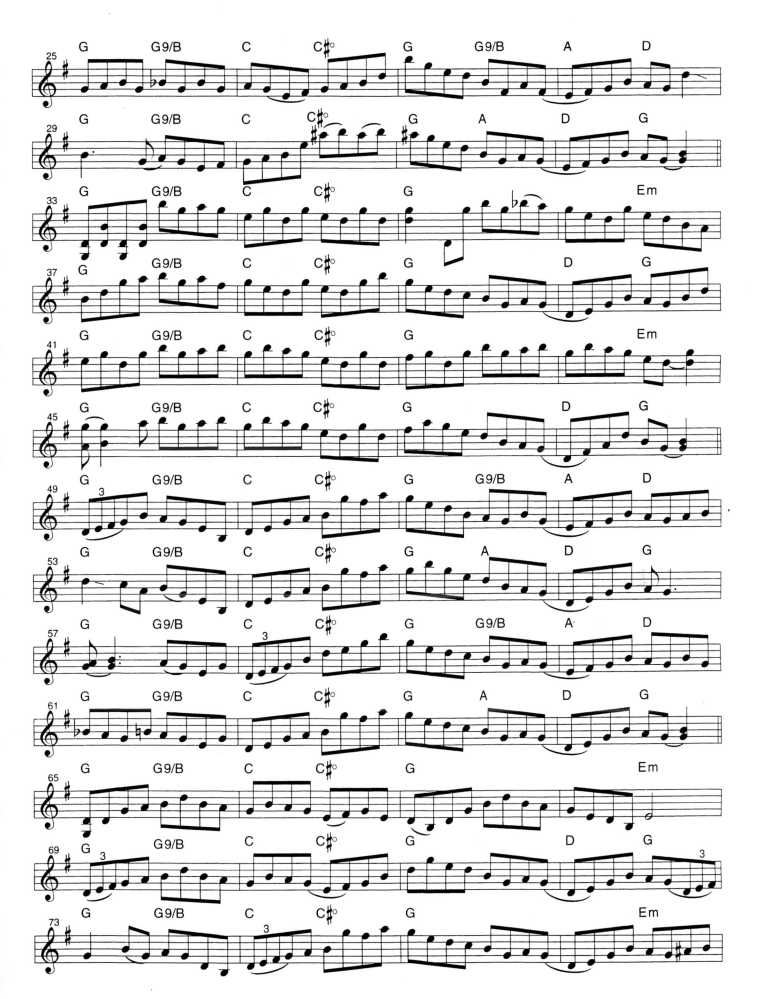

Salt River
Salt Creek

Old Time-Bluegrass-traditional

This is a two part tune played by bluegrass and oldtime fiddlers. Three variations on each section are given here.

Variations

Say Old Man

Old Time - traditional

This is a Tennessee version of *Say Old Man* with seven parts. Five of the parts are in E minor and two are in E major. A big ritard should be observed in the last two measures leading to the final harmonic E.

Snowflake Reel

Traditional

The unusual characteristic of this American tune is the use of the Bb chord in measures 11-12.

Soldier's Joy

Old Time - traditional

Soldiers Joy is one of the oldest tunes played by most American fiddlers. The early printed versions of the tune have the same notes as measures 1-16. The bowings have been added to emphasis the dance quality of the tune. Measures 17-32 give a simplified oldtime treatment which can be expanded upon by adding drone strings and other double stops and shuffle bowing.

Soppin' the Gravy

Hoedown - traditional

This is a contest style theme and variations approach to a sixteen measure tune. The only harmonic variation in the six parts is found in meaures 49-64.

Star of the County Down

Traditional Irish

Although this is a traditional Irish tune, it is included in this book because many American fiddlers play this beautiful melody. The eighth notes are even, not swing, as in most fiddle waltzes. A double stop arrangement is found in measures 33-64.

St. Anne's Reel

This tune is played by New England, Celtic and Southern American fiddlers.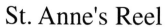
emphasises the dance lilt of the tune.

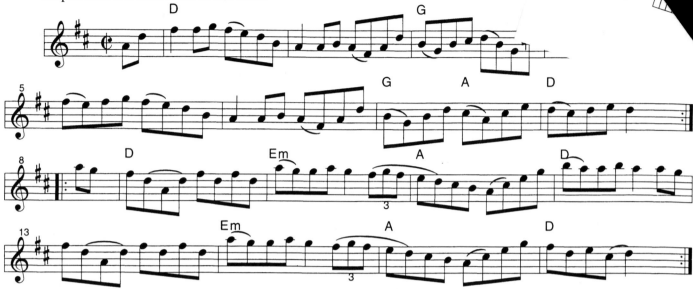

Stone's Rag
Lone Star Rag

Traditional

Texas and Western fiddlers call this tune *Lone Star Rag* and Southern fiddlers know it as *Stone's Rag*.
The eighth notes are played with a swing feel.

Stoney Point

Oldtime - traditional

...wo part fiddle tune has had other names. In fact, it appeared on a Flatt and Scruggs recording as ...*and Banjo*. Measures 19-50 add fancier licks to the standard tune.

Sweetheart Schottische

Traditional

A schottische is a round dance that requires the ryhthm of tunes such as this one. The *Sweetheart Schottische* is played with a very square feel. The dotted eighth sixteenths are not to be played as triplets.

Temperence Reel

Traditional Irish

The rolls found in measures 1, 3, 5 and 7 are typical of this style tune. It is played by bluegrass and oldtime players as well as traditional celtic fiddlers.

Texas Schottische

Traditional

Although there are many triplets in this tune, the dotted eighth sixteenths are played strictly, so that they do not sound like triplets. Measures 25-28 are played as as occasional interlude. The form as indicated by the repeats is ABABACA.

Tugboat

Contest Hoedown

This is a Texas contest tune. It has three sections with a final variation of the first part closing the tune.

Tom and Jerry

Contest breakdown- traditional

A contest hoedown warhorse, this tune is played by many fiddlers and has evolved into quite a showpiece. There are eight sections in this arrangement which are loosely based on either the first or second part. It is often played with Texas style accompaniment.

Washington County

Kenny Baker

Kenny Baker based this tune on the *Washington and Lee Swing*, a dixieland style tune from the early twentieth century.

Turkey in the Straw

Oldtime - traditional

Also known as *Old Zip Coon*, most American born people have heard this song of southern origin.
There are much fancier ways to play it, however, many times simplest is best.

Twinkle Little Star

Traditional

The traditional melody to this old time tune is found in the first 32 measures. Measures 33-64 add a
hybrid of bluegrass and contest licks.

137

Under the Double Eagle

John Phillip Sousa

Originally written as a band march, this tune has become a fiddling standard. The tune is often played without the introduction and the fourth section, which is in Bb. All of the parts are in this arrangement which ends with a final statement of the second part, or main theme.

Wagoner

Tennessee Wagoner

Measures 33-48 present a Texas contest style variation not found in the original two part tune. When performing *Wagoner* as an old-time tune, this section should be omitted.

Wednesday Night Waltz

Waltz - traditional

The main theme is found in measures 1-32 in a tricky double stop arrangement. A low octave variation appears in measures 33-64. A final high octave variation is found in measures 65-96.

Westphalia Waltz

Waltz - traditional

This popular tune is played by contest, bluegrass and square dance fiddlers. It has two 32 measure parts, ending in measure 64. Measures 65-128 give additional variations. The bow should be lifted in measures 33, 34, 41, 42, 97, 98, 103 and 104 to allow the strings to ring during the rests.

Whiskey Before Breakfast

Oldtime - traditional

This tune became a standard in the fiddle repertory during the past twenty five years. It is a standard two part form played with variations. This is the basic melody.

Year of Jubilo

Civil War Era Traditional

This simple two part tune is often played without repeats. It is performed at a march tempo. The "Year of Jubilo" refers to a year in which all debts are put aside.

Wild Fiddler's Rag

This arrangement is based on Howdy Forrester's recording of this own tune.

Howdy Forrester

Wild Fiddler's Rag
Texas Contest Style

Howdy Forrester

Mark O'Conner's high intensity contest style performance is the basis for this arrangement of Howdy's tune.

Yellow Rose Waltz

Waltz - traditional

This two part contest waltz is full of fiddling turns and licks. The repeat may be omitted to shorten the tune.